T0129519

The Journey
Ask me I was there

Dianna Shroads

WestBow
P R E S S
A DIVISION OF THOMAS NELSON

WestBow Press books may be ordered through booksellers or by contacting:

WestBow Press
A Division of Thomas Nelson
1663 Liberty Drive
Bloomington, IN 47403
www.westbowpress.com
1-(866) 928-1240

Because of the dynamic nature of the Internet, any web addresses or
links contained in this book may have changed since publication and
may no longer be valid. The views expressed in this work are solely those
of the author and do not necessarily reflect the views of the publisher,
and the publisher hereby disclaims any responsibility for them.

Any people depicted in stock imagery provided by Thinkstock are models,
and such images are being used for illustrative purposes only.

Certain stock imagery © Thinkstock.

ISBN: 978-1-4497-8143-9 (sc)
ISBN: 978-1-4497-8144-6 (e)

Library of Congress Control Number: 2013900085

Printed in the United States of America

WestBow Press rev. date: 1/21/2013

Edwin "Who" Shroads

12/24/49–12/14/08

The Journey

"In the beginning"—that's how God says it. In the beginning, thirty-eight years ago, I chose a man to love, to honor, and to cherish for as long as we both might live with God's help. We needed Him—oh, how we needed Him. Today is February 9, 2009, and I need to write this down before the shadows of my memory take away the awesomeness of this journey.

Married in Pearl City, Hawaii, and traveling the continents and islands because of military assignments, my husband, Eddie, and I were joined together as a team. Sometimes he got the assignments, but often I got the mission. The meeting place was Colorado Springs, but his proposal took us to his home in Hawaii.

We spent the night of our wedding at the beach (Houbuch) with his family. It was the very place he had grown up and spent his time surfing and becoming a man. Houbuch was a special place for us. Each time we visited Hawaii, we always returned for treasured moments there. It was a very intimate place. Often no words needed to be spoken between us as we peered into the vastness of the Pacific together; the language of our hearts was understandable. At times, the waves were mighty. At other times, they kissed the shore ever so tenderly.

I would return one day, thirty-eight years later, to bid my last aloha to my beloved.

In 1978, on that very island, I was introduced to the Savior of my soul, Jesus Christ. Shortly thereafter, a very nice lady gave a prophetic word: "Eddie will do great things for the Lord." As she shared this message, all I could think was, *The best thing he can do is get saved.* Little did I know the implications of that statement.

Early in the morning of December 13, 2008, I left the house with the car loaded to accomplish two very important tasks. I had scheduled two special decorating events. In the morning, I spent several hours decorating for a major event at the MPEC in Wichita Falls. Sisters in Christ was having their annual Christmas banquet that night, and they expected over one hundred folks. For lunch, I had scheduled a special graduation luncheon for Tasha Tippet at the home of her grandparents. Decorating, food coordinating, and overseeing the gathering of friends for these events were honors for me. (Tasha is my pastor's daughter, and she has been very special to me since her childhood. My daughter, Janelle, chose to have her sing at her wedding as a gift of gratitude to Tasha for the love she had already shown our family.)

After I completed Tasha's luncheon, I returned to the MPEC to finalize the decorations. I had chosen angels as the theme for that year's event. (Thank you, Donna Sikes, for sharing your great collection with me for this special night.) About 4:30 p.m., I left to go home and get ready for the event. When I arrived, my husband was busy in the kitchen fixing snacks for the football game he was preparing to watch. I had about an hour or so before I needed to return to the MPEC. Eddie was fine and relaxed and recommended I take a power nap before I returned to participate at the banquet.

When I was ready to leave, Eddie told me I looked nice, kissed me good-bye, and told me to have fun. (That moment would become a treasured memory for me.)

Upon my arrival, I watched as each guest came and filled the room. The most honored guest was unseen, yet most welcome. During praise and worship, I felt compelled to kneel down and worship the Lord for all He had done and for all that He is. While kneeling, I saw off to the right an outline of an angel picking up something very tenderly. I quickly wondered if my request to have a pre-visit to heaven would be granted since I had been thinking about folks who had visited heaven and come back to tell of their experiences. But the words to the songs of worship called me back to the praise being lifted from our hearts to God.

The evening was very intimate. The speakers shared their messages of honor to the Lord Most High, and the fellowship was sweet among everyone there. The prayers were faith filled, and all who came were touched by the Master's hand. He met us in that room. Folks lingered because of the presence and the peace that reigned there.

Around 11:15, I arrived at home tired, satisfied, and ready to unwind. As I entered the bedroom, however, I saw my husband lying on the floor. My first thought was that his back might be hurting, and I went to him to check. When he did not respond, I immediately dialed 9-1-1. The voice on the other end of the phone talked me through CPR until the fire department arrived. I remember trying to follow the techniques given, but I was so emotional that I wasn't sure whether I was even following the process right.

The paramedics followed the sound of my voice back to the bedroom and began to take over. The policeman who came in with them took me to the living room and began asking questions. My neighbors, Pat and Shirley, arrived and supported me emotionally as I answered questions and waited until the paramedics took my husband out on the gurney to the ambulance. Then I quickly changed clothes and went outside to follow the emergency vehicle, which was still in the driveway. When I asked why they were not moving, someone said, "We have to get him stable before we can move him."

He's still with us, and they're going to get him through this, I thought.

They left shortly thereafter, and we followed the ambulance as closely as possible to the hospital.

When we arrived, the attendant placed us in a family room. Our other neighbor, Brandon, came in shortly. A beautiful nurse came too and shared the power of trusting in God during such a time. She was so gentle and very compassionate. It wasn't long until the doctor came in and sat down. He was very kind as he said, "You did everything you could until the paramedics arrived. They also did what they could. So did I, but he did not make it."

I remember feeling a bit lightheaded as he spoke, and words came out of my mouth: "Lord, You promised." A peace came over me that hasn't left me—even through today. I remember listening to the doctor as he explained that he did not know the cause of death. Probably more than six minutes passed before I found Eddie lying there. I began to tremble on the outside as he spoke, but deep inside I felt a peace that I knew was supernatural as God took over.

I asked if I could see Eddie. The doctor replied, "Because he was in good health and we don't know for sure what he died from, the coroner will have to release him before you can go in. But as soon as possible, you should get to see him."

The doctor left the room, and the nurse returned and spoke to me tenderly about her recent loss and how she had fully relied on God to see her through that time. Shortly thereafter, the hospital chaplain came and asked if I wanted anyone called. I requested my pastor, and he and his wife, Linda, and their daughter, Tasha—whose luncheon I had attended to earlier in the day—were there before I was able to go back to see Eddie. Everything seemed so perfectly aligned, though things happened in a speed unrecognizable by the standard measure.

Pastor Gary began with prayer as he joined us. Then soon a nurse arrived to take me back to see Eddie. I asked whether anyone wanted to go with me: Pastor Gary and Linda chose to do so. The others decided to remember him as they had known him. They waited there, supporting me in prayer. The nurse took my arm, wrapped her arms tightly around mine, and took one step at a time with me. She talked to me and supported me with strength, standing as close as she could. I felt her confidence that I could face whatever was before me.

As we entered the dimly lit room, I saw a nurse over in the corner. She said, "He's ready for you, and I kept him warm. You can stay as long as you want."

I sat beside the bed and talked for a while. Pastor Gary sat right beside me. I remember saying things I thought the kids would like to have said. Then something came up from deep inside me. I reminded Eddie that God had written in His Word that "the women received their men back from the death.

"God," I said, "if You ever were going to do anything, now would be a good time to do it."

When I didn't get the response I was waiting for, I just talked for a while longer. When I was satisfied, I got up to leave and squeezed Eddie's toes as I usually did when I woke him up in the mornings.

It was a pretty long walk back down that hall, and Tasha was waiting for me. With tears in her eyes, she hugged me. I told her to remember to love lots and because I was scheduled to be her wedding decorator in January, I assured her I would still be there for her—just as she was there for me. I added that it would give me something to look forward to.

Poppy and Shirley and our neighbor, Brandon, were waiting to escort me home, and that's where I wanted to be. It seemed that if I could just put my head under the pillow and wake up again, everything that had happened would turn out to be just a dream.

Shirley told me she'd stay with me for the night, but I really wanted to be alone and she honored that. When everyone was gone, I sat alone on the couch and began to think about what was ahead of me. I realized I needed to tell the kids: Jenny lived in Hawaii, Jason in Nevada, and Janelle in Alaska. That was very difficult, and I knew they'd be on their way as soon as possible. Family is so supportive at such times, and I thank God that each of them had spouses to help them feel less lonesome. Remarkably, however, I never felt alone during the whole event.

The phone rang about 2:30 as I was still sitting there. It was the coroner's office. The gentleman asked several questions, which were quite like the ones the police officer had asked earlier. Then he added that under the circumstances an autopsy needed to be preformed. Because Eddie had been healthy and no one was home during his collapse, they needed to confirm the cause of death. He also added that during the initial testing they would know right away if it were a heart attack. I asked if they had to do an autopsy, and he shared that it was procedure. The circumstances made it mandatory.

Physically, I felt a bit tired. I headed to bed. But sleep didn't come, and my mind began to run ahead of me. I knew I needed to get up. I am a journalist by nature, and I write my thoughts very frequently. Pen in hand, paper poised and ready, I began to write the story of Eddie's life—as I saw it.

Who's on First?

Early on, in Hawaii, Eddie began his

passion for being a team member .

And he lived it out all the days of his life.

Little league, on the ball fields of Hawaii, were

the starting point for his journey of a lifetime.

His dad, Jacob Shroads, instilled in him these words:

"Son, if you can't play good, at least look

good. Then with practice, you get good."

Eddie practiced, encouraged by all his Ewa

teammates and family members.

They cheered him on. They themselves

were a vital part of the game.

He grew in stature as a man, and he grew

with gifts of integrity and compassion for

those wanting to enter into the game.

He had a heart as big as a stadium but a focus

that helped him keep his eye on the ball.

"Swing batter, batter!"

And he would swing,

getting better with each of life's curveballs,

the risers, and fastballs, too.

The pitches were thrown, and he decided to

serve his country in the US Air Force.

Proud—ready and leaving his first home—

he began the games of his lifetime.

He played in parks of Colorado, Germany,

all over Europe, Texas,

Guam, and of course in all of the Pacific places he could.

He was good at the game.

He once told me,

"Honey, it takes an hour to play the game

but two or three to unwind."

He was so intensely focused, but those unwinding

times are where the real story lies.

His was a team sport, and most of the practices

and training took place at the tailgates of

a convoy of vans and trucks in the parking lot.

The fellowship that took place there was

greater than any you might imagine.

Those team members

looked out for each other,

took time to stop the hurried life,

and they really got to know each other as they

built a team of

"Hall of Famers in their eyes."

This training carried over into Eddie's family

life and time at his workplace.

You can take the boy out of Hawaii, but I realized

you can't take Hawaii out of the boy.

I learned this as I watched him play game

after game wherever we went.

His team of friends are world-wide. Every place he went, he drew folks into becoming a part of the team. The training and the practices were all worth it.

I found myself a little jealous at times because he was so good at his sport. I knew he was in a very special league of his own.

Folks, like the Wichita Falls Ohana—meaning "Family"—would gather in our home no matter where we were stationed. They'd stay until the wee hours of the night and often into the next day.

The game went on as new teammates were placed on the roster. All it took was an introduction by someone already on the team. Each one reaching one was how this team was developed.

Through the seasons of our lives, folks
came and went. Some even
tried other sports, but they always played the game by these
simple instructions from one of the greatest
coaches in my hall of fame.

Once I figured out some of the plays, I
cheered for the team, watching
for the victory sure to come, and I recognized
Eddie's real talent. It wasn't in the
things you'd notice right off. It just kind
of developed as he taught the game.
Therein laid his secret.

You see, everyone was invited to join, but there was a test.
Could you be a "team" player?
Were you willing and ready to look out
for the others and share your time?
Could you be faithful to show up for practice?
Would you be on time and ready for the game?

Times proved many were, and the hall of Famers grew.

Every seat filled.

Bases loaded.

Games were tied.

Pitches were thrown.

Batters would swing.

The crowd would roar.

A true home run.

All happened because Eddie kept his eye on

the ball and his heart in the game.

Once, while playing a game on the Big Island

of Hawaii, Eddie heard the line up called.

One by one lots of big, long Hawaiian names were called.

Then came Eddie's turn to be announced.

"And on second base is Eddie Shroads."

"Eddie Who? What kind of Hawaiian name is that?"

the announcer said. And the crowd laughed.

But the game had been announced. "Eddie

'Who' Shroads" was playing for his

Hawaii team, and they were headed for a win.

The name stuck like bubble gum on

the bottom of a stadium chair.

Time marched on and some of the team

members went on before him.

His good buddy "Slick."

His coach named "Ray."

Their games were called.

Just think about it …

"Swing batter, batter!"

The pitch is thrown.

The ball connects.

It's out of the park!

With a home run in sight, Who's on first. Slick

rounds second, and Ray's calling the game.

Yes, it's out of the park! Eddie kept his eye on

the ball, and he followed it skyward.

So will the other trained teammates,

One by one.

Make sure you keep your eye on the ball.

Keep your heart in the game.

Don't forget to show up for practice.

Know this, GOD picked you alone for this team.

Get your name on His roster, and you'll one day

hear the game of your life being called.

For now,

sign up.

Look good.

Show up for practice.

You'll get better with time.

The greatest coach of all gave Eddie first-hand training.

You see, Eddie said, "Coach, sign me up!"
His coach's name was Jesus.
That very moment he was placed on the
heavenly "Hall of Fame Roster."

Yes, Jesus coached him.
Taught him to look good.
Stayed with him during practice.
And Eddie got better with time.

As he listened, he heard these words:
"Batter up! Swing batter, batter!"
Life's pitches were thrown.
Connections were made.
And he was out of the park and
into the arms of Jesus, who
welcomed him "Home."

My prayer is for you today.

Jesus, we need you now. Keep this team together

so that the stadiums up there will be filled.

Every seat! Lord, cheer us on that each of us might

find our names on the roster of all rosters,

The Book of Life.

All you've got to do is ask Him. Say,

"Sign me up!" He's done the rest.

Jesus took the wooden cross—it was made of the same

material as were the first bats—and He got for us

the most famous home run of all time.

He's cheering you on.

So get your heart in the game.

Keep your eyes on Him.

Get to practice.

He'll take care of the rest.

Eddie, we'll see you soon.

Love you always.

Your wife, Diana

Feeling empty of the words that had so easily flowed, I paused. Then I heard in my heart, "that's not all." I wondered what that could possibly mean, and then I remembered the banquet I had attended the previous night. I had seen an angel pick up something: my husband, heading home.

I had waited thirty-two years for this to happen. In fact, many years back, I had spent three days fasting and praying for Eddie's salvation. I had a vision of him alone on an island. Nothing around him was alive. It was as though everything was charred, as on a volcano site after an eruption. In that vision, he was very desperate and cried out: "What do you have that I don't have?"

I watched from a distance, invisible to him. I said, "You know His name. Just call His name."

Again he shouted, "What do you have that I don't have?"

I replied with my same response, and the vision ended. Somehow I knew someday he would do that very thing.

At another event during a Sunday morning service, I was very discouraged and needed someone to pray for me. I walked to the front of the church, and Pastor Wilburn began to pray for me. During the prayer I closed my eyes and saw Pastor Wilburn fade away. Jesus was standing there in his place. His hands were on His hips, and He grinned. He said, "I promised you that you and your whole house will be saved. What do you have to worry about? Get on with My business. I'll take care of the rest of them. There is much to do, and you need to go do it."

Then—just as easily as the picture had become clear—I saw the Lord's face fade away. Pastor Wilburn was standing there finishing up his prayer.

These events are more than memories; they are reminders of promises fulfilled.

The peace that I felt was contagious. Folks would come to the house to console me, and they would end up leaving with smiles. Our best friends, Frank and Ladonna Lagat, and Joyce Beam brought their love along with many others. (When God steps in, He does the miraculous. It floods the whole atmosphere with His presence.) Janelle and Kurt were the first to arrive from Anchorage. She shared that she had cried the whole way, but when she saw my peace and joy, her sadness lifted. I can't tell how good it was to have family and my other children on the way. Folks came and went, and the love they poured forth was never ending. I felt embraced by the hands of God. He was propping me up on every leaning side. The words I had prayed many times over others came back to me a hundred fold.

The ball team hit a home run with our family. They were some of the first folks to arrive at our home. The word had spread fast and far, and folks were so precious to us. Our friends and family were scattered beyond the borders of Texas, even over the oceans. But our home was lavished with food, with supplies, and with the presence of folks who knew how to connect. They, just as a team should, came together to encourage and to bring a touch to this journey that managed to accomplish God's will perfectly.

I needed someone to read "Who's on First." TK said he knew someone who could do it. He suggested Cutter who had "been to college" and "can read." I roared with laughter.

You see, you have to know this team. They are the greatest teddy-bear-like and marshmallow-hearted folks who give great hugs. On the other hand, they carry big swords (disguised as ball bats) to protect all those that are a part of the team.

I asked if I could meet Cutter and ask him myself.

"Sure, the Game Warden can do it," TK replied.

I thought, *This is a fellow I really need to see to be sure.*

What happened next in the journey is dear to me, and I'll be forever grateful. Cutter came over; he is a gentle giant of over six feet in height. I knew that if nothing else, folks would pay attention just because of his size. Later I found out that his heart is just as big as he is.

I sat with Cutter as he read silently. "Mrs. Who, this is him, this is really him. Everything. It's just like him," he insisted.

"I know," I replied. "I lived with him for thirty eight years, and that's the man I love."

"That's him all right," he said, "It'll be an honor to read this for you."

"Cutter," I said, "it's one thing to read it to yourself. It's a whole different ball game to stand in front of folks and have your heart in the game. Will you read the story out loud for me? This is a pretty big job, and I don't want you to feel uncomfortable if you can't do it."

He stated that he'd take it home and practice. He would come back to read it to me because he wanted to say it just the way I would. This he did faithfully, returning the next day and crying as he read the words aloud to me for the first time. I knew he could do it because his heart was ready. He had the assignment, and I prayed for his confidence. He didn't let me down.

Sometimes even the best plans require adjustments. TK came back later and stated that he had thought of someone else who could read the "Who's on First" story. He said, "The Rev can do it. He preaches and such, so I think he could do you a good job."

I inquired about the person, whose real name was Hutch. He was indeed a reverend.

"TK," I said, "I already asked Cutter, but there's a possibility that Hutch could help him." I needed to talk to Cutter about it first.

TK went on to explain that Hutch was not only a reverend but was also part of the honor guard. That really brought a smile to me because we were planning on having an honor guard perform the flag ceremony during the service. When TK heard that he said, "I think Hutch would do that for you. I'm not sure of his schedule, but I'll let him know.

God had His fingerprints on the event long before the journey began. Our youngest daughter, Janelle, had been a good friend with Hutch's wife, Dana, throughout her high school years. I was in awe of the purposeful planning of God and was really touched when I found this out. (I had even sat with Hutch's little daughters at a few ball games while Eddie and Hutch played on the ball field.) As I watched God unfold His story before my eyes, I realized that He had seen to the details of my journey. I still stand in awe of how much He cares for us. We are to Him of far more value than are feathered sparrows or the lilies of the field.

TK and Larry did indeed come back the next day with the ball team. They reported that Hutch was going to lead the honor guard for my husband. The second step of honoring his military service, then, would be completed right behind the words Cutter would speak. Next, I needed someone to help with talking about the *Ohana*, or family. Then I needed a speaker for Eddie's Civil Service time.

Because I had never been to a memorial service, I didn't know what to expect. I chose to organize the ceremony around his life, his USAF Military Service, our Ohana of Hawaii, his Civil Service, and softball. The details were placed before me, and the friends who would have the honored places of sharing their words during the service stepped up to the plate.

I asked a wonderful lifelong friend of our family if he would speak to us about Eddie's growing up years in Hawaii. Les Marquin blessed us so wonderfully with his memories. Jim Guillespe, Eddie's last supervisor, accepted the honor of speaking about Eddie's impact on the students that came through Sheppard AFB. A very special friend of mine, who also happened to work with Eddie, was asked to sing "Amazing Grace." She gladly accepted. Lisa Sanders, another lady who is a very special lady to me, had spoken at several ladies' events through the base chapel and Sisters in Christ. She is a living picture of the virtuous woman, and I admire her greatly. Lisa added a very special touch to the service and was able to acquire a three-foot picture of Eddie from a smaller one I had in the bedroom. It captured the grin he wore every day. Our family had it placed in a tropical flower arrangement for the service.

Playing ball in Hawaii where Eddie got the nickname,"Eddie Who".

*Eddie with his sister Linda, hubby Terry, sister-in-law Gail
and brother Jim and his mom Esther Shizue Shroads*

Friends Les and Diane Marquin who spoke at the memorial.
Les and Eddie grew up together in Ewa Hawaii.

*Julie and Orchid Williams, best hawaiian family
fans ever. Orchid is our god-daughter.*

Frank and Ladonna Lagat, Eddie's hawaiian brother
and sister. Joshua and Kayla the keiki's.

Eddie stole second base along with our hearts.

"Swing batter batter."

The ball field memorial. Each player was given sand to put in their pockets from the beach we were on when we spread Eddie's ashes. During fifth inning each team member gathered around 2nd base and emptied their pockets of the sand. "Swim-bra-woosh" was the herald shout. Many winning games were closed with that sound. This team was filled with winners.

"' Jenny, Jason, and Janelle our children. JJJ and Company

He did not "always" wear ball clothes.

Aloha til we meet again on the other shore.

The day of the Memorial service in Wichita Falls TX.

The Lord had us propped up on every leaning side the day of Eddie's memorial. I saw folks I had not seen for a long time and friends that had walked with us through the journey of the past week. These were treasured times. God was in control, and I could not have made it without Him.

The directors ushered us into the service as the songs from IZ played. I heard, "Starting all over again is gonna be rough, but we're gonna make it" and "In this life I was loved by you." Jason led us into the service, and my precious sister-by-love loaned me my brother, who escorted me. My sons-by-love followed with Jen and Janelle, and they looked so sharp in their USAF uniforms as their wives leaned on their strength-filled arms. I am very proud of each of them.

Pastor Gary led our service in prayer. As always, the Comforter of all comforters was there. I still felt the same supernatural peace I had received in the hospital waiting room. Cutter was the first to speak, and he blessed me as he shared the words I had written. As he stepped off the podium, I rose to embrace him in gratitude.

"I just got my name on the Roster," he said to me.

I was overcome with joy. I knew God had handpicked this man not only to support me but also as a means of touching his life as well.

As a song about worshipping with the angels played, I knew that Eddie was doing just that. I'm sure that if God let him look through the portals of heaven he could see the folks impacted by his life and that the knowledge would bless him. Next, Les—a friend anyone would love to have for life—spoke from the Ohana standpoint. (He knows how to laugh, and that is what he and Eddie did well together.) Les took us back to ole' Hawaii and shared some boyhood memories of Eddie that left grins on our faces and brought a dash of laughter for our futures. Then IZ's "Somewhere over the Rainbow" played, reminding me that somewhere, someday we'll have the opportunity to see things from God's point of view. Until then, I hope and pray more will join the team and get their names on "The Roster."

Pastor Gary spoke about the intimate things we as a family had shared with him. The Tippitt family has blessed us so richly throughout the years, and our paths were very similar. I sensed it was a tender time for Pastor because he knew Eddie personally, and I prayed for him to be strengthened as he shared his stories. Lisa Sanders touched heaven with "Amazing Grace," and that is what we have been given. She gave her offering of love, and through her song I was filled with an amazing sense of God's arms reaching out to each of us, bidding us to come closer to Him. The truth of the passage, "All you who are weary and heavy laden, come, and I will give you rest," was being proclaimed through the words of her anointed song. Lisa sang to an audience of One and made a throne of praise for the King of kings. You see, Lisa worked with Eddie, encouraging him daily and bringing us to the Father through her prayers often.

This section of the service ended with the song that says, "In this life I was loved by you." "If it all falls apart, I will know deep in my heart, the only dream that matters has come true and in this life I was loved by you."

Jim Gillespie spoke about Eddie's military career. He gave me insight into the magnitude of folks he had helped while living out his daily schedule. Eddie truly had a servant's heart; further, he had compassion for the new airmen and their families that helped put them at ease. Charlie, Michelle, Sharita, Sully, Darla, Jim, Lisa, and so many others teamed together—not just for our family— but for the thousands of folks that need support, and I will be forever grateful. May God richly bless you for the servants' hearts you have; they reach the nations.

The United States flag of red, white, and blue was presented before us with such honor and pride, representing Eddie's service to the nation. This banner also represents those military members who one at a time and together as a team working shoulder-to-shoulder protect and provide for the nation's citizens. (It brings to mind the banner over me mentioned in God's Word: love. And I feel that the love our military members have given through the years is woven into the pattern and fibers of each flag.) We stood in honor as the flag was opened, folded, and presented.

Hutch came to me with the flag folded in his arms. His eyes were fixed, and tears brimmed as he presented me with a memorial of a job well done. As he leaned forward and recited words he has said many times to other families, I realized that he too was one of Eddie's friends and his heart was heavy. Proud, bold, and with a tenderness I can't explain, I took the flag and held it close to my heart. I knew the nation has been blessed by God's amazing grace.

Later, as Hutch visited with us at the home, he shared that the flag ceremony was the toughest thing he'd ever had to do because Eddie was his friend.

Often, I have seen folks receiving flags on television and thought of the pain a person receiving such a flag must feel. Never had I focused on how the person presenting it might feel. My prayer is for an open heart to encompass all God is doing and to be a minister to all who are hurting.

The doors opened and the airmen proceeded forward into the open air, marching step-by-step as a clock's ticking. Ready, aim, fire, and twenty-one signals were given from their guns. As the doors were closed and our family members made their way down the aisle toward the back of the room, I saw faces that shared their joy of the journey and a tender awareness of the time we will be apart from Eddie. But we will remember that with each passing day, we are closer to being together again than ever before.

Eddie gave me many memories during his lifetime. I choose to share them because he taught me how to love. As our story continues, the treasured moments will make the journey easier.

Christmas of 2008

The twenty-fifth of December was fast approaching. It was only four days away, and we needed to get Jason back to his family for Hanukkah and Christmas. Mimi and Brooklynn were going to meet us in Hawaii for the Sea Side Memorial. During this time, I found a moment alone in the house and felt compelled to put in a video. I had several choices to select from, but I picked "Rain" by Rob Bell. I had previously watched some of his videos and knew that they usually run about fifteen minutes. The teaching is very thought-provoking, and his presentation is gentle.

The video began as Rob and his one-year old son went for a walk through the woods and around a lake. Theirs was a very special dad and son time. Rob rejoiced over the fact that he and his son had time together. During their walk, about halfway around the lake, it began to cloud up. Thunder crashed and lightning flashed, and it was getting very windy. Rob reached back and put his son's hood on for him so that he wouldn't get wet. Then he put on his own hood.

As Rob was walking as quickly as he could, he heard his little boy screaming at the top of his lungs. The small son took off his hood and looked for his dad. He couldn't see his face because of the hood he was wearing. He said, "Where are you? I'm afraid!"

I could identify. I wanted to know when my life's storm would pass, and I really needed to see my Father.

Rob stopped, reached around, and took his little boy in his arms. He held him tightly and told him, "I've got you, buddy. I love you. And I know the way home." Over and over Rob repeated those words. As he spoke, I found myself in the arms of my Father, and He was saying the same thing to me.

Later, Rob stepped out of the woods and shared that someday his son might sit in therapy asking, "Dad, why did you let me go through that?" Rob said he would be crushed if that happened because he would do anything—anything at all—to protect his son. "When you needed me most," he would tell his boy, "I got to hold you close. I got to tell you that I love you, and I got to tell you that I know the rest of the way home. I hold that memory as one of the most intimate, precious times of our lives."

"I love you, Daughter, and I will always love you. I've

got you, and I know the rest of the way home." That was exactly what my Father was saying to me through that video. I knew I had asked to see my Father's face, but He had let me see His heart.

During the Christmas season, folks came and went and there was tenderness everywhere. I even told a few people that "Eddie gets to spend Christmas with Jesus, and I'm jealous." That usually brought a smile. What lay ahead of us was looking better every day.

Aloha means I love You

arly on the morning of December twenty-six, I began my day in prayer as always. I realize, in hindsight, that the Lord had placed a particular prayer request on my heart. I remember asking for one more confirmation that Eddie was in heaven. I recalled the promises in Scripture, and I remembered my vision of the angel. Still, I just wanted God to tell me one more time that Eddie had made it safely home. I prayed, "Lord, if he's really there, let me fly first class." That thought was God given. I had purchased tickets and knew we were flying coach and was very comfortable with that plan, but God another idea in mind.

It was the day after Christmas, and we all headed for the airport. Jen and John and Aubrey left on a flight before the one Kurt, Janelle, and I would board. We waited in line to check in, and at the counter we were told that our flight had been delayed for three hours. We would be placed on another flight so we could make our connection in Arizona.

Kurt took the tickets from the agent, and we headed to check in. I carried the documents for transporting Eddie's ashes, which were inside the suitcase I carried. When we reached the first area of customs, I presented my ID and ticket as well as the paperwork that allowed me to transport Eddie's remains. The agent behind the podium took my documents. Then, just as easily as possible, she stepped from behind her podium and gave me a hug. No words were exchanged, but the gesture reminded me that God was still holding me.

We proceeded to the place where they scan luggage. I put my suitcase in the bin, and away it went through the tunnel. I stepped through the scan machine and waited at the end of the x-ray machine. The lady took a very long time studying the suitcase's contents. I turned to the agent behind me and said, "I think she may need these documents."

That lady, also a TSA agent, very gruffly stated, "We don't need anything you have. Just move down like you are being told."

At this time, Kurt was standing to my right and Janelle to my left. Janelle began to cry because you don't mess with her mama! Kurt, on the other hand, said, "Mom, if you will let me, I'll take it from here." And he did just that.

He gestured to another TSA agent behind the X-ray

scan screen and gave him the documents. The gentleman apologized, and then he told Kurt he would need to take the remains out of the suitcase so that the item might be scanned individually. Very gently, he did just as he said. Janelle had not seen the box with the remains inside until that time because I had very carefully protected them and didn't want to cause any undue sorrow. When she did finally see the box, the tears began to flow. Tenderly, we waited and held each other until the ordeal was over. Then we headed to board the plane.

As God would have it, we were in the walkway and headed for the plane door when Kurt looked at the tickets to tell us our seat numbers. "We have first class seats!" he shouted in an excited voice.

I stopped! I turned to Janelle and said, "If you ever doubted where you daddy is, God just shouted. He used Kurt to tell us! I prayed this morning for a sign, and God just gave it to us. Dad's in heaven!" Neither of them had known of the prayer I had prayed earlier in the morning.

We stepped up to the door of the plane, and the attendant said, "Ma'am, you need to check that suitcase. There is no more space on board for it."

"Sir," I replied, "I choose not to check it because I have my husband's remains in it."

Again he said there was no room, but he allowed me

to try to find a spot. If I couldn't, the bag would have to be checked. It was then that I sat down in first class, in the first seat.

With concern in his voice, the attendant asked, "Is that your seat?" When I said that it was, the color faded from the man's face. He said he would move his own suitcase and store mine in its place. By that time, Janelle and Kurt had moved into the seat behind me; the suitcase fit perfectly in the overhead bin above them.

The plane took off, and I noticed a gentle man in the seat beside me. He read a book in which the pages seemed to never turn. That was my cue to not talk to him.

God really does things right. When the attendant had served the passengers, he came to me and asked, "Ma'am, why didn't you want me to check your baggage? Were you afraid we would loose it?"

"No sir," I replied. "You see, I just have a little longer with my husband, and I'd just like to keep him as close as possible."

With that, the attendant knelt down on the floor beside me and began to share some of his heartaches as a husband and talked of his true love, his wife. We spoke for quite some time. The gentleman sitting at my right was listening in to the whole conversation, not saying a word and not turning a page in his book. Before we left the plane, I knew I had planted in the attendant spiritual seeds that would change his life forever. He was headed down the salvation road to Jesus.

Just before we landed, I headed for the restroom. The ride grew so turbulent that I felt like a piece of popcorn tossed in a hot machine. I bumped around everywhere and had to recover finally as I made it to my seat. The gentleman next to me spoke for the first time. "Picked a fine time to go, didn't you?"

His words made me smile, and I realized his book was on the same page it had been on when we took off. He had indeed been listening. To this day, I'm not sure if he was praying about or just listening to and the conversation he overheard. Only God knows the possible impact.

God announced our arrival in Hawaii.

Afte r we arrived at the airport and made it home with Jen and John, every light on the whole island went out. It was quiet; it seemed we could hear God breathe. He turned on the stars and shut up the noise so we could just be a family. Everyone was gathered together in Jen and John's home, and the peace of God fell like a mantle over all of us. This act of divine love and preparation bonded us together in a way I will never forget. We slept in peace in that home, sheltered as we rested in His care.

Family is precious, and each person within it brings spice to the shared table. I knew that Eddie had always wanted to go back to the beginning place of his childhood, fulfilling the full circle of God's plan for him. Eddie had spent many of his younger days at a beach called Houbush. He surfed and spent time with friends and family there. Houbush was also the very beach where we—along with all of his family—spent our wedding night. It is also the place we visited with our children as they were growing up, gathering with many of the family and friends we met along the way. Even Eddie's grandmother used to go with us to that very place to sit and pick seaweed.

Memories from that place are special, and so were the times when just Eddie and I would go alone and look out across the vast ocean. Together we made memories of our lives during the tender times on that beach. I remember standing beside him there when first his father passed away and then again when his mother went home. Words were expressed through our hearts during that time. It was a very special place, and he always said he'd like to return there. I planned to make it his final resting place as he had requested.

During the next day, Eddie's brother called and said he'd found a place where we could spread Eddie's ashes. He had a friend with a boat, and he also had a friend with property that went out to the shoreline. In addition, he mentioned that he had located a friend who had a jet ski. On another note, he said that the time I had chosen for the ceremony would not work because it would be dark by then, and the road to Houbush was not good anymore. I felt as though he had said these things so fast that I'd had the breath knocked out of me. "I'll get back to you on this," I politely said and ended the conversation. His plans didn't settle with me.

I shared with the children everything Jimmy had shared and waited for their reply. Jenny said we should call Cousin Jo and have him go check. Jo and Elizabeth lived on the side of the island where Houbush was located. They promised to go look and call us back.

Later in the day, Jo called and explained that everything I wanted was available on the site, even adding that there was a small ballpark there. He said the beach was beautiful. The sand was soft, and the waves gently kissed the shore. He also said he'd checked the sun setting time, and it would go down at 6:06 on Sunday. Other than having acquired a few new potholes, the road to get there was very much as I had described to him from my memory.

The kids were elated by what Jo had reported, but we still had one hurtle to go over. Jim had shared that we needed to be a hundred yards offshore to spread the ashes, and I knew a boat was out of the question. So was the jet ski.

My awesome son spoke up. "Mom, I know how to take Dad out, and I can do it."

I asked what he was thinking. Apparently, he had wisdom beyond understanding, and I knew where he got it.

"Mom, I'll take him out on a surfboard. That's where he surfed, and I'd like to do that for him."

I was overwhelmed by his generous offer and asked a simple question, "Will you promise me you'll come back?"

"Yes, Mom, I'll come back. I promise. The details were in place, and the journey to fulfilling Eddie's last requests was quickly coming to fruition.

Our cousin Kathy Abe graciously accepted our invitation to be the minister for the ceremony. I called family members and scheduled for Sunday afternoon at five on Houbush beach and proceeded to thank God for all He had done again. Julie and Jay had seen to it that we had leis for the occasion. Aunties had picked flowers for us to share at the shore. During the day it had rained, and there were clouds in the sky upon our arrival.

It was the perfect backdrop for God's finger paints. The sea was gentle, and the beach only had a few fishermen on the shore and just a sprinkling of folks spending time together. The family and friends began to gather for our final aloha.

Kathy began the ceremony with a prayer, thanking God for all the love we have been privileged to experience during this time. She also asked for His presence to abide in this special place and time. Brian Ponce sang one of Eddie's favorite songs in Hawaiian. The lyrics translate this way: "Let me walk through paradise with You, Lord. Take my hand and lead me on." Brian has been a friend of the family for many years, and we were blessed to have him and his beautiful bride, Kathy, there as part of the fond farewell.

Stanley, Kathy's husband, shared the history of Eddie's life. Then Jason, John, and Kurt read the "Who's on First" story, changing the name from Edwin, to "Dadwin," as it had originally been written. I was honored that they did such a great job. Jason began with tears in his heart that overflowed down his cheeks as the two centurions, John and Kurt, came along side of him for support. I could not have been more proud of the men in my life who stood before me. The girls—Jen, Janelle, and Mimi—had helped me pass out leis and were holding the little ones with great tenderness. When Jason, Kurt, and John finished reading, Kathy again said a prayer. Then we walked down to the shore.

We placed the ashes in Jason's hands and put leis around his neck before he paddled out. Farther and farther he went into the ocean's perfect place just beyond the last wave. Then he gave a toss of ashes that formed a rainbow with the leis quickly following in salute of the Aloha that will be etched in our minds and hearts forever.

We waved from the shore as Brian sang songs of fond farewell that we all felt in our hearts. We tossed our flowers into the shallows, and they floated out toward the deep. Some returned to tell us we would be reunited again someday. God used His canvas to color in His presence, and the backdrop was beautiful. There stood Diamond Head in the background. The sun reflected on it from behind us, shining on the water and directing Jason's journey back to the shore. The sky was vibrant with colors more vivid than the darkness that could have overshadowed this time. God placed a red cloud from heaven to the sea, letting us know the bridge had been completed. Any of us were welcome to climb that ladder into His presence by doing what Eddie had done. We too could call out His name.

We gathered again to embrace Jason and walked through the sand, up the hill to have one final word. Kathy gave me the opportunity to explain why I had chosen this special place for our gathering. I shared with family members and friends the life stories that had taken place on that very beach. I told them of the love that began on our wedding night, and I talked through the time that I myself had called out to God for my salvation. I shared the love we had together as family, bringing to mind our memories of family gatherings right on that very spot. I reminded my children of their early days there with Great Grandma Momoyo Shimizu, when they had watched her pick seaweed. I reminisced how Eddie and I, as husband

and wife, had come to this very place as a refuge when the sadness of a lost loved one had billowed over us.

Then I invited each listener to have his or her new beginning on that beach if they had not already done so. I told them of how simple it is to just call His name. Jesus was waiting, watching, and ready to receive each of them. I asked them not to delay because we don't have tomorrows promised. I saw the smiles of folks who already had called out to the Name above all names. I saw the tears of those who at that moment wanted to begin again. And I saw the peace on my children's faces because each of them knew the Truth and had called that very Name. Each face had its own response to being able to call out.

I ended with a prayer for peace and joy to fill our lives. Then I shared Mary Jane's words of wisdom: "We will have holes in our lives where he is not present, but we will not fall into them."

We ended the ceremony with Brian's rendition of "Aloha Oi."

As we looked out into the ocean, we saw a lone surfer who never turned around. He just sat on his board. To the right, there was a large sea turtle playing in the sea. The sun kissed the horizon, and the stars began to shine as the moon took its rightful place. Then we as a family had a picnic on the beach and fellowshipped together late into the evening just as we had so many times before.

Return to Normal by God's standard

U pon arriving back in Wichita Falls, I knew I'd be going back to work. I was surprised at the treasure I had waiting for me there. I was welcomed with lots of hugs as precious little ones told me they missed me, but one event will stand out as extra special. Brad Dalke, a fifth grade student, came into the office with a beautifully wrapped gift. He said, "Mrs. Shroads, I have something for you. I hear you been going through a hard time."

I got up and walked around my desk to where Brad stood. I asked him what was in the bag he had brought. "It's a rock," he replied.

I collect rocks from all around the world as a point of contact when I pray for the nations. Brad has brought me several from his travels. I opened the box and before me was a beautiful ceramic rock engraved with Psalm 37:24. It also said, "Hold on child, I got you, Love God."

I began to wrap my arms around Brad as I cried. I

then shared the story from the Rob Bell video, explaining about how God had said to me essentially the very same thing then. "I've got you. I love you. And I know the rest of the way home." Brad smiled as he left the office. I was truly blessed through the love of that little boy.

After he left, I read the card. It contained a beautiful story about two friends. At different times during their lives, they left notes for each other on the windshields of their cars. They were simple notes to remind one another that they were being thought of and prayed for and would often include an invitation to spend time together.

One day, one of the friends died. In the grieving, the one left behind thought aloud, *God, I'll never receive a note on my windshield again, I miss my friend so much.* Such a simple truth reflected the magnitude of the depth of love the friends had had for each other.

The next morning, the friend went out to her car. There on the windshield was a leaf. She heard a still, small voice say, "I left you a note." She smiled as she picked it up and knew she was being thought of. The next day her car was almost completely covered in leaves. Then she knew that God had left her lots of notes, many times. Each one was precious.

I looked up and thanked God for all He had done through the arms and hearts of the friends who had been surrounding me. I called Brad's mom the next day to tell her of the happening in the office, and her reply brought me to happy tears.

She shared that Brad had come home and explained that he got to hug Mrs. Shroads. "I hugged her longer than I ever hugged my sister," he reported. He had been touched by the story also. I thanked God again for the gentle ways He finds to make me smile.

Time does pass, and friends came and went, but a very important event took place almost two months to the day of Eddie's home going. I had been invited to go to dinner with my best friend, Joyce, and her hubby, Jim. Two precious friends from North Dakota joined us in celebration.

During dinner I was asked to share my testimony of what had happened. As I concluded my story, Mike began to share of when they heard of Eddie's death. They had prayed for our family. Mike said, "I heard the Lord speak these words—" then he began to cry, a very deep cry. I could almost feel the depth of his pain.

For a long time he sat there sobbing, trying to compose himself so that he might share with me the message he had heard. "God said," he finally reported.

" 'I've got her where I want her.'"

I sat in awe of those profound words. I didn't fully understand their meaning, but I knew I was being held. God loved me, and He knew the rest of the way. All I had to do was lean into Him, and He'd take care of all of the details.

Mine has been a journey never to be forgotten. I am glad I wrote down the details as I remember them. As time goes on, I know they will fade. For now, I am still walking with God. And forever I am blessed.

He has me, He loves me, and He knows the rest of the way home.

I am glad you took the time to go with me on this journey. I am forever grateful for the opportunity to share this story with you.

As I recall the love, joy, and laughter shared through this time, I will always remember your friendship. Your name may not have been mentioned within these pages. But know this: God knows who you are, and you were used in a very awesome way to make the journey easier.

May the Lord keep you and make His face to shine upon you. May He lift up His countenance to you and give you peace.

In His Service all the days of my life.
Mrs. Diana "Who" Shroads